Small Life

poems by

Karol Nielsen

Finishing Line Press
Georgetown, Kentucky

Small Life

Copyright © 2022 by Karol Nielsen
ISBN 978-1-64662-969-5 First Edition
All rights reserved under International and Pan-American Copyright Conventions. No part of this book may be reproduced in any manner whatsoever without written permission from the publisher, except in the case of brief quotations embodied in critical articles and reviews.

ACKNOWLEDGMENTS

I would like to thank the editors of Finishing Line Press, Leah Maines and Christen Kincaid, for publishing my chapbook. I'd like to thank the editors for publishing the following:

Anti-Heroin Chic—"Charlie's Angels," "Watch TV and Hold Hands," and "Painting and Poetry"
Conestoga Zen—"Dream," "Watch TV and Hold Hands," and "Painting and Poetry"
The Dribble Drabble Review—"Judy's Advice"
Fine Lines—"New Yorker" and "Painting and Poetry"
Gingerbread Ritual—"Lunch Hour"
Global Insides (Chalant Publishing)—"Small Life"
Global Poemic—"Cop Shows"
Lion and Lilac—"Judy's Advice" and "New Yorker"
Lockdown Literature (CultureCult Press)—"Spring Quarantine" and "Cop Shows"
Poetry and Covid—"Spring Quarantine," "Cop Shows," and "Teacher"
The Raconteur Review—"Judy's Advice"
Retirement Plan—"Dream," "Topless," "Fur Coat," "Do You Have the Time?," and "Dog Walker"
Prachya Review—"Small Life" and "Spring Quarantine"

I am grateful to Judith Mary Gee and Katherine Dering for writing beautiful blurbs for this chapbook; my sister, Cynthia Nielsen, for shooting my author photo; and my parents, Alan and Linda Nielsen, for everything.

Publisher: Leah Huete de Maines
Editor: Christen Kincaid
Cover Art: Karol Nielsen
Author Photo: Cynthia Nielsen
Cover Design: Elizabeth Maines McCleavy

Order online: www.finishinglinepress.com
also available on amazon.com

Author inquiries and mail orders:
Finishing Line Press
PO Box 1626
Georgetown, Kentucky 40324
USA

Table of Contents

New Yorker 1

Judy's Advice 2

Watch TV and Hold Hands 3

Charlie's Angels 4

Poetry and Painting 5

Lunch Hour 6

Do You Have the Time? 7

Dream 8

Topless 9

No Pants Subway Ride 10

Fur Coat 11

Dog Walker 12

Spring Quarantine 13

Small Life 14

Cop Shows 15

Teacher 16

NEW YORKER

I remember the Peruvian band in the subway station when I first moved to New York. I stopped and listened and it was magical. I was so green then that a man on the subway platform said, You're not from New York. I wondered how you acquired New York cool. I watched the city for clues. I saw a man with a rainbow Mohawk in the East Village, a man in a miniskirt wearing lipstick near New York University, and shirtless muscled men in the West Village. The city is more muted now, but it still offers clues. I was struck by the tall woman with pink and purple curly hair by Union Square and the petite young man with braided gray extensions on the subway. I have lived most of my adult life in the city, but my new colleague recently said, You're not from New York. I keep looking for clues.

JUDY'S ADVICE

Judy told me a story about a writer who drew a picture of her ideal man. She and her mother went looking for him. They found him in a bar. He was illiterate but he looked like her drawing. So she married him. Judy always says I could meet someone anywhere—the pharmacy, the grocery store, anywhere. I told her I went to a bar and had a Chardonnay. The man next to me wanted to buy me a drink. I said thank you but no. He persisted but my answer still was no. He was a gray-haired senior with a round belly and missing teeth who settled for a handshake. We didn't get married.

WATCH TV AND HOLD HANDS

He stopped on the train platform in front of me and stared menacingly. He was silent. Then he said, Let's watch TV and hold hands. I turned to the man and woman beside me on the bench, but they had no response. When he walked away, I noticed the tear in his pants around the ankle. He paced back and forth several times before two police officers walked him off the platform. Soon my train arrived and I headed home for Thanksgiving. After I arrived, I told my father what happened and we laughed. My father said, Well that will be a new poem. And I said, It's already done.

CHARLIE'S ANGELS

He used to call out Charlie's Angels when I passed by him at the entrance to the subway where he sits on a crate with a cup in his hand. I was hoping he might say it again since I had lost most of the weight I gained from too many cheeseburgers and donuts. But still he stared ahead without noticing me. Then, on my way to a poetry reading, he perked up and said, How are you, Charlie's Angels?

PAINTING AND POETRY

On my way to work, I walk by a young woman who sits on the sidewalk outside my office. Her cardboard sign says, I lost everything except my hope and smile. My colleague said she lives in a shelter in New Jersey and comes to the city to beg. Her cup for donations rarely has more than a few coins. She usually does a crossword puzzle, but sometimes she paints water colors, abstract shapes and the city skyline. In the afternoon, she sells her paintings across the street. I used to have intense fear of ending up homeless when I am too old to work. My father retired a few years ago and he says that his life turned out far better than he ever imagined. It gives me hope that mine might, too, but if I do lose my home I won't paint. I'll write poems instead.

LUNCH HOUR

I was on my lunch hour in a deli with seating for customers. It was late in the afternoon and nearly empty. I almost skipped lunch because I'd had a donut for breakfast. But I couldn't bear the day without a break so I bought an iced coffee and slowly sipped it while reading Mary Oliver poems about birds and nature and the divine on my Kindle for iPhone. Its small screen fit the poems perfectly. Suddenly I was inspired to write my own lines even though I didn't have a poem.

DO YOU HAVE THE TIME?

He asked me for the time so I pulled out my cellphone which doubles as a watch and told him the time. He was an older man who seemed a little slow. Then he asked me where I was going. I said I was going to work. It was just across the street. He asked if he could walk with me. I said I was in a hurry. "But you're walking so slowly," he said. It's true that I was moving slowly. I had strained my back while sitting in a big chair telling my manager that a colleague sent harassing messages to me. She accused me of taking the man's point of view in relationships because I said I split the bills. I was the only one in the office who tolerated her and now that was over. Of course I didn't go into the complicated backstory with the man. I just told him I'd hurt my back. Well, this is my office, I said. He grabbed my arm and kissed my shoulder and I went on my way.

DREAM

I rarely remember my dreams. I have worried that it is a blow to my creativity but it is what it is. Even when I wake up in the middle of the night during a dream I forget it by morning. But I remembered one dream. I dreamed that I couldn't remember the name of Ken's girlfriend. I scanned my memory and Betty popped up. But in my dream I remembered that Betty Rubble was a character in the *Flintstones*. Not right. So I dreamed that I googled Ken's girlfriend. Then I woke up and instantly it came up me. Her name was Barbie.

TOPLESS

I was walking in Central Park on a hot summer day when I looked ahead for the vendor who sells me iced tea. I spotted a young woman and thought, Whoa, her shirt is so sheer! She was walking with an older man who could have been her father. As she got closer, I realized she was topless. I emailed my parents about the sighting and my mother posted the story on Facebook. My sister chimed in that it's legal so women can breast feed in public. I had seen topless women on foreign beaches but never in the city. Suddenly I felt provincial for finding it such a funny surprise.

NO PANTS SUBWAY RIDE

On my way home from a poetry reading, I noticed a group of men in their underwear. It was the middle of winter but it was an unusually warm, spring-like day, so at first I mistook their underwear for shorts. I hurried up so I could get a closer look. Yep, definitely underwear. I followed behind and watched them enter a bar with a crowd of men in their underwear. One man provocatively wore sheer black underwear. Later I learned that it was the annual No Pants Subway Ride, started as a joke by an improv comedy group. Participants take off their pants before their subway stop and, if asked why, they say they were getting uncomfortable.

FUR COAT

When I got off the train, I spotted a man in a rabbit fur coat on the subway platform. He was tall and the coat stretched down to his ankles. I thought of my grandfather who used to hunt. I went out with him once when I was little and he shot cottontails in the snow. When I grew up, I never wore fur. Once, when I worked on Park Avenue, my boss asked to borrow my wool coat. She had to take the subway and she worried protesters would spray paint her fur coat. I felt like a servant helping an upper class lady. She never asked again.

DOG WALKER

I saw a white poodle with bright pink fur on top of her head and around her ankles. She looked like a princess, a show dog, as a man held her on a leash by Central Park. It reminded me that I almost became a dog walker. After I interviewed, I went on a trial run with the owner, but the dog barked and growled and wouldn't come out of the cage. I didn't hear anything for months. Then the owner's wife offered me an early morning shift. I'd broken my arm in a car accident and told her what happened. She said let's wait until your arm heals. I found work as a writer instead but I still think about that job when I see dog walkers with packs of dogs, out there, rain, snow, or shine.

SPRING QUARANTINE

Spring came as the virus spread and most days I left quarantine at my parents' house in Connecticut to walk through the neighborhood, delighted by blooming magnolias, apples, forsythia, cherries, dogwoods, azaleas, daffodils, bluebells. I watched buds on maples, elms, oaks turn into lush leaves. I counted the walkers, runners, and bikers, about a handful to two dozen, saying hello as I passed by, and I wondered how long it would be before I got back to New York, to the life I had before the pandemic.

SMALL LIFE

My world is small now. I wake up at daybreak and have two iced coffees with my mom and dad in a wooded suburb in Connecticut. I work remotely, writing specialty occupation visa application reference letters for software developers, computer systems analysts, electrical and electronics engineers, financial analysts, marketing managers. I take breaks and go for long walks along my childhood running route. When I finish work, I watch the news and streaming TV series and movies with my parents who are retired. I write daily diary entries on my phone and sometimes I come up with a poem. I used to be inspired by random encounters in the city but now I have to find inspiration in my very small life in quarantine.

COP SHOWS

We watch cop shows one after another during the long hours of quarantine. *CSI: Miami* looked good because it starred an actor from a favorite series, *NYPD Blue*. The show opens with a grizzly murder or the discovery of a corpse and the suspects quickly emerge. It's full of beach and pool parties, bloody postmortems, cheesy lines, and unbelievable confessions. Too often I pick up my cellphone and check messages, social media, even the news, and lose the thread. But I always hope that the next episode will draw me in.

TEACHER

I started teaching creative nonfiction writing a few months before the September 11 attacks. That day I emailed all my students to make sure they were okay. One woman said her boyfriend worked in the twin towers but he took the day off to surf on the Jersey Shore. My mother shared her advice about teaching before I started: Love your students, she said. She spoke from the heart as a Sunday school teacher who treated her students like family. It came naturally to love my students as I nurtured their writing from often thin first drafts to well developed and sometimes published works. Because of the pandemic, I now teach online, but I look forward to the day when I can get back to the classroom, loving my students as I share insight about my deepest passion.

Karol Nielsen is the author of the memoirs *Walking A&P* (Mascot Books, 2018) and B*lack Elephants* (Bison Books, 2011) and the poetry chapbooks *Vietnam Made Me Who I Am* (Finishing Line Press, 2020) and *This Woman I Thought I'd Be* (Finishing Line Press, 2012). *Black Elephants* was shortlisted for the William Saroyan International Prize for Writing in nonfiction in 2012. Excerpts were honored as notable essays in *The Best American Essays* in 2010 and 2005. Her full-length poetry collection was shortlisted for the Terry J. Cox Poetry Award in 2021 and was selected as a finalist for the Colorado Prize for Poetry in 2007. Her work has appeared in the anthology *The Moment: Wild, Poignant, Life-changing Stories from 125 Artists and Writers Famous & Obscure* (Harper Perennial, 2012) and many publications, including *Epiphany, Guernica, Lumina, North Dakota Quarterly, Permafrost,* and *RiverSedge*. As a journalist, she covered Latin America, the Middle East, New York City, and other beats—contributing to Janes and Thomson Reuters magazines as a staff writer and editor, *New York Newsday* and the *Stamford Advocate* as a freelance writer, the *New York Times* as a stringer, and many others. She teaches creative nonfiction and memoir writing with New York Writers Workshop.

www.ingramcontent.com/pod-product-compliance
Lightning Source LLC
LaVergne TN
LVHW041526070426
835507LV00013B/1856